TOOLS FOR CAREGIVERS

- **F&P LEVEL:** C
- **WORD COUNT:** 40
- **CURRICULUM CONNECTIONS:** animals, habitats, nature

Skills to Teach

- **HIGH-FREQUENCY WORDS:** a, big, has, is, it
- **CONTENT WORDS:** chews, ears, fluffy, hair, hears, hello, legs, llama, long, neck, reaches, runs, tail, teeth, thick, warm
- **PUNCTUATION:** exclamation points, periods
- **WORD STUDY:** /k/, spelled ck (neck, thick); long /a/, spelled ai (hair, tail); long /e/, spelled ea (ears, hears, reaches); long /e/, spelled ee (teeth)
- **TEXT TYPE:** information report

Before Reading Activities

- Read the title and give a simple statement of the main idea.
- Have students "walk" through the book and talk about what they see in the pictures.
- Introduce new vocabulary by having students predict the first letter and locate the word in the text.
- Discuss any unfamiliar concepts that are in the text.

After Reading Activities

Llamas have long ears to hear, long legs to run, and long necks to reach grass to eat. What other things do llamas have that help them? Ask each reader to draw their favorite animal. Have them label the animal's body parts. What does each part help their favorite animal do? Have each reader present their animal to the group.

Tadpole Books are published by Jump!, 5357 Penn Avenue South, Minneapolis, MN 55419, www.jumplibrary.com

Copyright ©2024 Jump!. International copyright reserved in all countries. No part of this book may be reproduced in any form without written permission from the publisher.

Editor: Jenna Gleisner **Designer:** Emma Almgren-Bersie

Photo Credits: GlobalP/iStock, cover; a_v_d/Shutterstock, 1; Vladimir Bolokh/Dreamstime, 2tl, 2br, 10–11; Eric Isselee/Shutterstock, 2tr, 6–7; Generistock/iStock, 2ml, 14–15; Wirestock Creators/Shutterstock, 2mr, 12–13; Angela N Perryman/Shutterstock, 2bl, 8–9; Big Joe/Shutterstock, 3; slowmotiongli/Shutterstock, 4–5; Stefano Buttafoco/Shutterstock, 16 (left); LouieLea/Shutterstock, 16 (right).

Library of Congress Cataloging-in-Publication Data
Names: Brandle, Marie, 1989- author.
Title: Llamas / by Marie Brandle.
Description: Minneapolis, MN: Jump!, Inc., (2024)
Series: My first animal books | Includes index.
Audience: Ages 3–6
Identifiers: LCCN 2022054080 (print)
LCCN 2022054081 (ebook)
ISBN 9798885246705 (hardcover)
ISBN 9798885246712 (paperback)
ISBN 9798885246729 (ebook)
Subjects: LCSH: Llamas—Juvenile literature.
Classification: LCC QL737.U54 B73 2024 (print)
LCC QL737.U54 (ebook)
DDC 599.63/67—dc23/eng/20221110
LC record available at https://lccn.loc.gov/2022054080
LC ebook record available at https://lccn.loc.gov/2022054081

MY FIRST ANIMAL BOOKS

LLAMAS

by Marie Brandle

TABLE OF CONTENTS

Words to Know 2

Llamas 3

Let's Review! 16

Index 16

WORDS TO KNOW

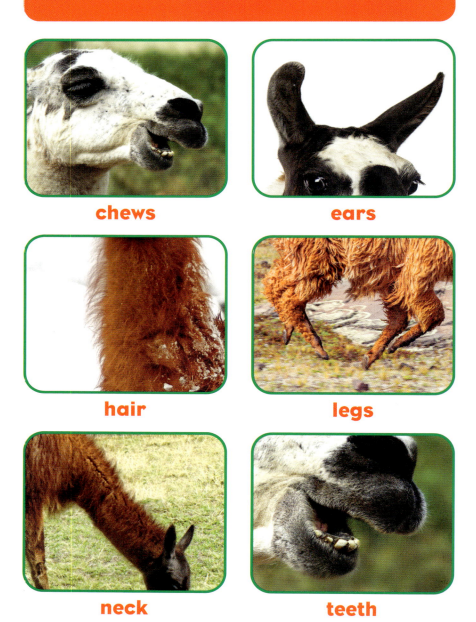

chews

ears

hair

legs

neck

teeth

LLAMAS

Hello, llama!

It has a fluffy tail.

ears

It has long ears.

It hears.

It has a long neck.

neck

It reaches.

It has big teeth.

teeth

It chews.

It has long legs.

It runs!

hair

It has thick hair.

snow

It is warm.

LET'S REVIEW!

Llamas can be different colors. What colors are these llamas?

INDEX

chews 11
ears 6
hair 14
legs 12

neck 8
runs 13
tail 5
teeth 10